# CAMPING JOURNAL

# FOR KIDS

# I'D RATHER BE ROASTING MARSHMALLOWS

## THIS CAMPING JOURNAL BELONGS TO

_____

# HOW TO USE THIS CAMPING JOURNAL

A camping journal is all about documenting your trips in a fun and unique way. This camping journal was set up to use 4 pages per trip, but you can use just two pages if you want.

The first and third page ask questions and get you thinking about your trip. A few questions can be answered by circling your answer. Questions with blank areas can be answered with words or pictures. Answer the question with whatever method works for you. Make this journal FUN. Make this journal about you and who you are.

The second and fourth pages are mostly blank. You can draw your own doodles of what you saw or did, or you can glue in items from your trip. Again, make this a fun journal. Add whatever you like.

## HERE ARE A FEW FUN IDEAS FOR THE BLANK PAGES

- Tickets (Bus rides, attractions, national parks)
- Maps
- Business cards from places you went or ate at
- Stamps
- Packaging from favorite candy
- Receipts
- Trip itinerary
- Park or campground brochure
- Pressed flowers, petals, or leaves from the local area
- Photographs
- Postcards

- Draw your favorite or most unique bug or animal you saw
- Draw the most interesting/unique thing you saw
- Places to visit, see, or eat at next time you go there
- Your packing list
- An item you wished you had packed
- Name of someone you met
- A collage of brochures from places you went or might like to go later
- Drawing of the skyline or of a mountain range you saw
- An autograph
- A cool bookmark
- A pressed coin
- An etching of a stone, raised street name, or a texture
- Local recipe
- Stickers
- Describe your campground
- What was your first thought when you arrived?
- Draw your favorite smell
- Grains of sand or dirt stuck to a piece of tape

CAMPING AT _____

CAMPING IN A

WEATHER REPORT

BEST PART OF MY DAY

_____

_____

_____

WORST PART OF MY DAY

_____

_____

_____

TWO THINGS I LEARNED

TODAY WAS

AWESOME    FUN    COOL    TERRIFIC
OKAY    BORING    EXHAUSTING

CAMPING DOODLE

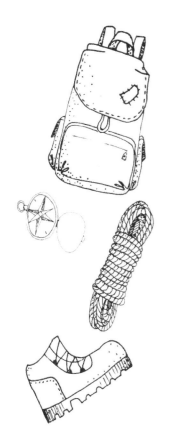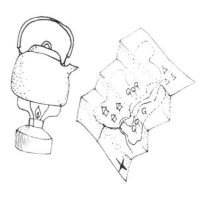

CAMPING AT _____

TODAY'S DATE

THREE THINGS I SAW TODAY

TODAY I ATE _____

AND IT TASTED  GREAT  AWESOME  HEAVENLY
              HORRIBLE  TERRIBLE  OKAY

IF I WENT HERE AGAIN I WOULD

_____
_____
_____
_____

WHO CAME WITH ME

_____
_____
_____
_____
_____

DRAW AN EMJOI TO
DESCRIBE THE DAY

THIS CAMPING TRIP IN A _____
WAS _____ BECAUSE I GOT TO

_____

_____

I GIVE THIS TRIP ☆ ☆ ☆ ☆

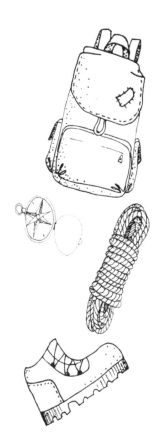

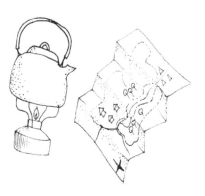

CAMPING AT _____

CAMPING IN A

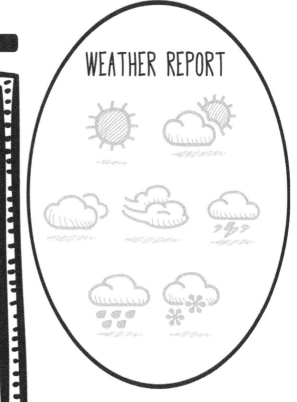

TODAY'S DATE

## WEATHER REPORT

BEST PART OF MY DAY

_____

_____

_____

WORST PART OF MY DAY

_____

_____

_____

## TWO THINGS I LEARNED

_____

_____

_____

_____

_____

_____

_____

## TODAY WAS

AWESOME   FUN   COOL   TERRIFIC

OKAY   BORING   EXHAUSTING

## CAMPING DOODLE

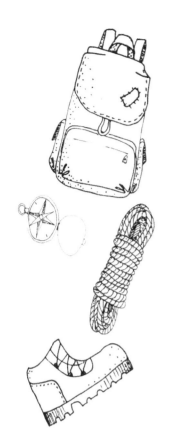

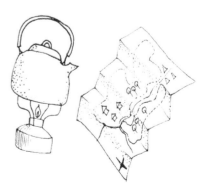

CAMPING AT _____

TODAY'S DATE

THREE THINGS I SAW TODAY

TODAY I ATE _____

AND IT TASTED   GREAT   AWESOME   HEAVENLY
                HORRIBLE   TERRIBLE   OKAY

IF I WENT HERE AGAIN I WOULD

_____
_____
_____
_____

WHO CAME WITH ME

_____
_____
_____
_____
_____

DRAW AN EMJOI TO
DESCRIBE THE DAY

THIS CAMPING TRIP IN A _____

WAS _____ BECAUSE I GOT TO

_____

_____

I GIVE THIS TRIP  ☆☆☆☆

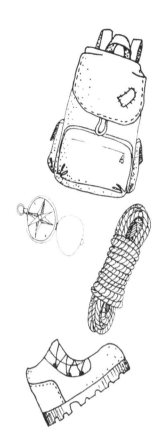

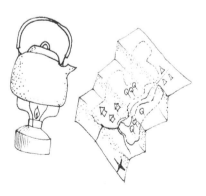

CAMPING AT _____

CAMPING IN A

TODAY'S DATE

BEST PART OF MY DAY

_____
_____
_____

WORST PART OF MY DAY

_____
_____
_____
_____

WEATHER REPORT

TWO THINGS I LEARNED

_____
_____
_____
_____
_____
_____
_____

TODAY WAS

AWESOME    FUN    COOL    TERRIFIC
OKAY    BORING    EXHAUSTING

CAMPING DOODLE

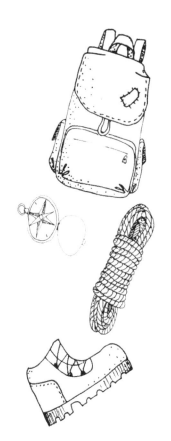

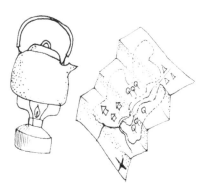

CAMPING AT _____

TODAY'S DATE

THREE THINGS I SAW TODAY

TODAY I ATE _____

AND IT TASTED   GREAT   AWESOME   HEAVENLY
                HORRIBLE   TERRIBLE   OKAY

IF I WENT HERE AGAIN I WOULD

_____

_____

_____

_____

THIS CAMPING TRIP IN A _____
WAS _____ BECAUSE I GOT TO

_____

_____

WHO CAME WITH ME

_____

_____

_____

_____

_____

DRAW AN EMJOI TO
DESCRIBE THE DAY

I GIVE THIS TRIP ☆☆☆☆

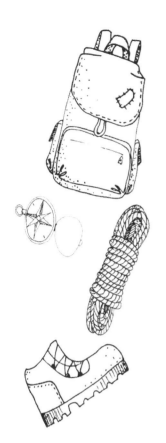

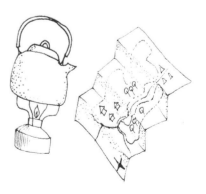

CAMPING AT _____

CAMPING IN A

WEATHER REPORT

BEST PART OF MY DAY
_____
_____
_____

WORST PART OF MY DAY
_____
_____
_____
_____

TODAY WAS

AWESOME   FUN   COOL   TERRIFIC
OKAY   BORING   EXHAUSTING

TWO THINGS I LEARNED

_____
_____
_____
_____
_____
_____
_____

CAMPING DOODLE

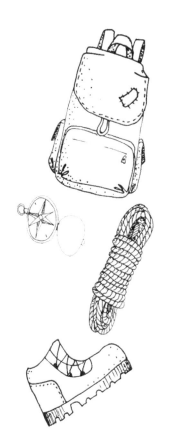

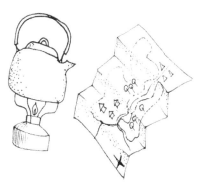

CAMPING AT _____

TODAY'S DATE

THREE THINGS I SAW TODAY

TODAY I ATE _____

AND IT TASTED    GREAT    AWESOME    HEAVENLY
                 HORRIBLE    TERRIBLE    OKAY

IF I WENT HERE AGAIN I WOULD

_____

_____

_____

_____

WHO CAME WITH ME

_____

_____

_____

_____

DRAW AN EMJOI TO
DESCRIBE THE DAY

THIS CAMPING TRIP IN A _____
WAS _____ BECAUSE I GOT TO

_____

_____

I GIVE THIS TRIP  ☆☆☆☆

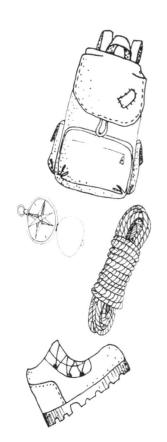

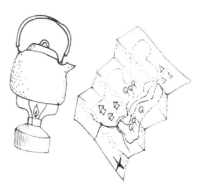

CAMPING AT _____

CAMPING IN A

WEATHER REPORT

BEST PART OF MY DAY

_____
_____
_____

WORST PART OF MY DAY

_____
_____
_____

TWO THINGS I LEARNED

_____
_____
_____
_____
_____
_____
_____

TODAY WAS

AWESOME   FUN   COOL   TERRIFIC
OKAY   BORING   EXHAUSTING

CAMPING DOODLE

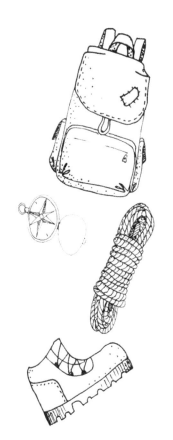

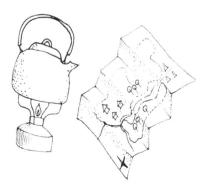

CAMPING AT _____

TODAY'S DATE

THREE THINGS I SAW TODAY

TODAY I ATE _____

AND IT TASTED   GREAT   AWESOME   HEAVENLY
                HORRIBLE   TERRIBLE   OKAY

IF I WENT HERE AGAIN I WOULD

_____

_____

_____

WHO CAME WITH ME

_____

_____

_____

_____

_____

DRAW AN EMJOI TO
DESCRIBE THE DAY

THIS CAMPING TRIP IN A _____
WAS _____ BECAUSE I GOT TO

_____

_____

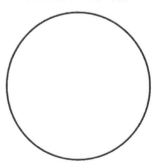

I GIVE THIS TRIP ☆☆☆☆

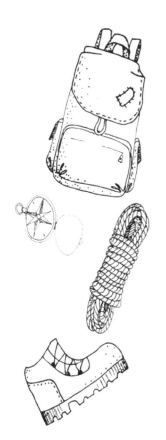

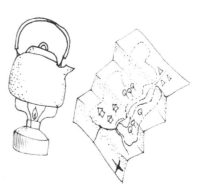

CAMPING AT _____

CAMPING IN A

WEATHER REPORT

BEST PART OF MY DAY
_____
_____
_____

WORST PART OF MY DAY
_____
_____
_____
_____

TWO THINGS I LEARNED

_____
_____
_____
_____
_____
_____
_____

TODAY WAS

AWESOME   FUN   COOL   TERRIFIC
OKAY   BORING   EXHAUSTING

CAMPING DOODLE

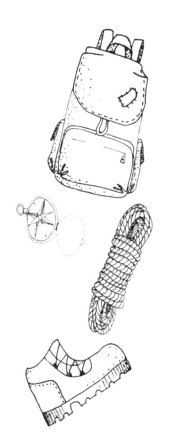

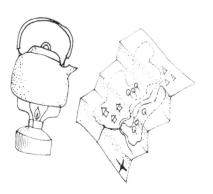

CAMPING AT _____

TODAY'S DATE

THREE THINGS I SAW TODAY

TODAY I ATE _____

AND IT TASTED    GREAT    AWESOME    HEAVENLY
                 HORRIBLE    TERRIBLE    OKAY

WHO CAME WITH ME

_____

_____

_____

_____

IF I WENT HERE AGAIN I WOULD

_____

_____

_____

_____

DRAW AN EMJOI TO
DESCRIBE THE DAY

THIS CAMPING TRIP IN A _____
WAS _____ BECAUSE I GOT TO

_____

_____

I GIVE THIS TRIP ☆ ☆ ☆ ☆

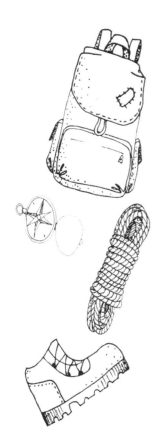

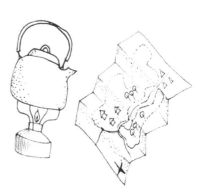

CAMPING AT _____

CAMPING IN A

BEST PART OF MY DAY
_____
_____
_____

WORST PART OF MY DAY
_____
_____
_____

WEATHER REPORT

TODAY WAS

AWESOME   FUN   COOL   TERRIFIC
OKAY   BORING   EXHAUSTING

TWO THINGS I LEARNED

CAMPING DOODLE

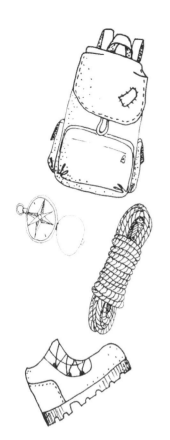

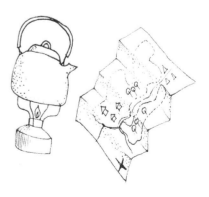

CAMPING AT _____

TODAY'S DATE

THREE THINGS I SAW TODAY

TODAY I ATE _____

AND IT TASTED   GREAT   AWESOME   HEAVENLY
               HORRIBLE   TERRIBLE   OKAY

WHO CAME WITH ME

IF I WENT HERE AGAIN I WOULD

_____

_____

_____

THIS CAMPING TRIP IN A _____

WAS _____ BECAUSE I GOT TO

_____

_____

DRAW AN EMJOI TO
DESCRIBE THE DAY

I GIVE THIS TRIP ☆☆☆☆

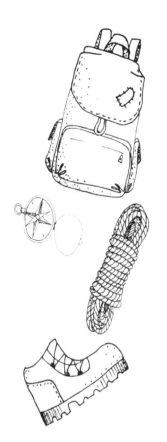

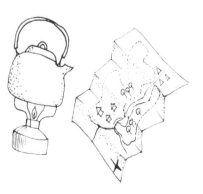

CAMPING AT _____

CAMPING IN A

TODAY'S DATE

WEATHER REPORT

BEST PART OF MY DAY
_____
_____
_____

WORST PART OF MY DAY
_____
_____
_____

TWO THINGS I LEARNED

TODAY WAS

AWESOME   FUN   COOL   TERRIFIC
OKAY   BORING   EXHAUSTING

CAMPING DOODLE

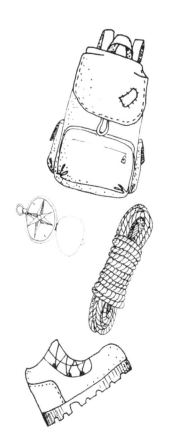

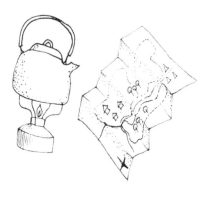

CAMPING AT _____

TODAY'S DATE

THREE THINGS I SAW TODAY

TODAY I ATE _____

AND IT TASTED    GREAT    AWESOME    HEAVENLY
               HORRIBLE    TERRIBLE    OKAY

IF I WENT HERE AGAIN I WOULD

WHO CAME WITH ME

DRAW AN EMJOI TO
DESCRIBE THE DAY

THIS CAMPING TRIP IN A _____

WAS _____ BECAUSE I GOT TO

I GIVE THIS TRIP ☆☆☆☆

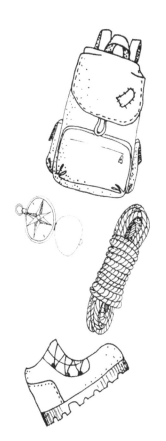

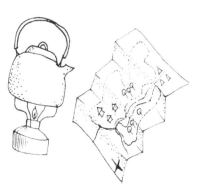

CAMPING AT _____

CAMPING IN A

TODAY'S DATE

BEST PART OF MY DAY

_____
_____
_____
_____

WORST PART OF MY DAY

_____
_____
_____
_____

WEATHER REPORT

TWO THINGS I LEARNED

_____
_____
_____
_____
_____
_____
_____
_____

TODAY WAS

AWESOME    FUN    COOL    TERRIFIC
OKAY    BORING    EXHAUSTING

CAMPING DOODLE

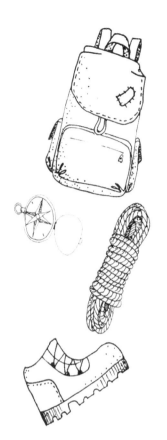

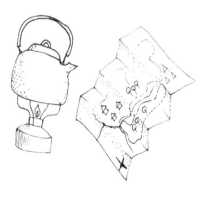

CAMPING AT _____

TODAY'S DATE

THREE THINGS I SAW TODAY

TODAY I ATE _____

AND IT TASTED   GREAT   AWESOME   HEAVENLY
                HORRIBLE   TERRIBLE   OKAY

IF I WENT HERE AGAIN I WOULD
_____
_____
_____
_____

WHO CAME WITH ME
_____
_____
_____
_____
_____
_____

DRAW AN EMJOI TO
DESCRIBE THE DAY

THIS CAMPING TRIP IN A _____
WAS _____ BECAUSE I GOT TO
_____
_____

I GIVE THIS TRIP ☆☆☆☆

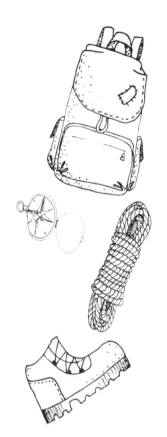

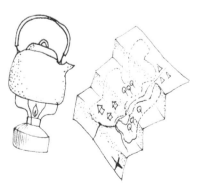

CAMPING AT _____

CAMPING IN A

BEST PART OF MY DAY
_____
_____
_____

WORST PART OF MY DAY
_____
_____
_____

WEATHER REPORT

TWO THINGS I LEARNED

_____
_____
_____
_____
_____
_____
_____

TODAY WAS

AWESOME    FUN    COOL    TERRIFIC
OKAY    BORING    EXHAUSTING

CAMPING DOODLE

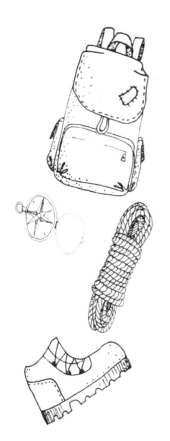

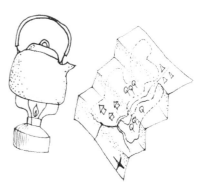

CAMPING AT _____

TODAY'S DATE

THREE THINGS I SAW TODAY

TODAY I ATE _____

AND IT TASTED    GREAT    AWESOME    HEAVENLY
HORRIBLE    TERRIBLE    OKAY

IF I WENT HERE AGAIN I WOULD

WHO CAME WITH ME

DRAW AN EMJOI TO
DESCRIBE THE DAY

THIS CAMPING TRIP IN A _____
WAS _____ BECAUSE I GOT TO

I GIVE THIS TRIP ☆☆☆☆

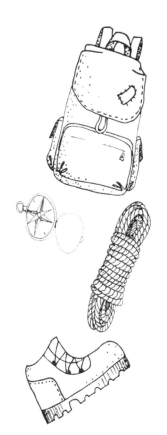

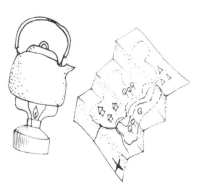

CAMPING AT _____

CAMPING IN A

TODAY'S DATE

BEST PART OF MY DAY
_____
_____
_____

WORST PART OF MY DAY
_____
_____
_____

WEATHER REPORT

TODAY WAS

AWESOME    FUN    COOL    TERRIFIC
OKAY    BORING    EXHAUSTING

TWO THINGS I LEARNED

_____
_____
_____
_____
_____
_____

CAMPING DOODLE

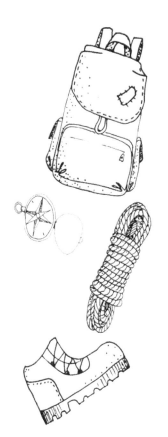

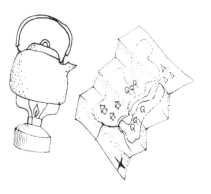

CAMPING AT _____

TODAY'S DATE _____

THREE THINGS I SAW TODAY

TODAY I ATE _____

AND IT TASTED  GREAT  AWESOME  HEAVENLY
               HORRIBLE  TERRIBLE  OKAY

IF I WENT HERE AGAIN I WOULD
_____
_____
_____
_____

WHO CAME WITH ME
_____
_____
_____
_____
_____
_____

DRAW AN EMJOI TO
DESCRIBE THE DAY

THIS CAMPING TRIP IN A _____
WAS _____ BECAUSE I GOT TO

_____

_____

I GIVE THIS TRIP ☆☆☆☆

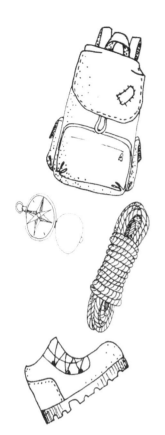

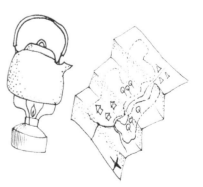

CAMPING AT _____

CAMPING IN A

TODAY'S DATE

WEATHER REPORT

BEST PART OF MY DAY

_____
_____
_____

WORST PART OF MY DAY

_____
_____
_____
_____

TWO THINGS I LEARNED

_____
_____
_____
_____
_____
_____
_____

TODAY WAS

AWESOME   FUN   COOL   TERRIFIC
OKAY   BORING   EXHAUSTING

CAMPING DOODLE

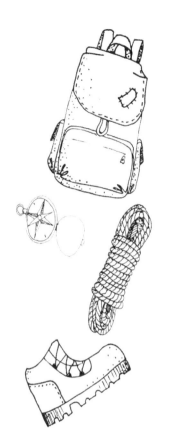

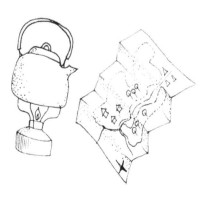

CAMPING AT _____

TODAY'S DATE

THREE THINGS I SAW TODAY

TODAY I ATE _____

AND IT TASTED  GREAT   AWESOME   HEAVENLY
               HORRIBLE  TERRIBLE  OKAY

IF I WENT HERE AGAIN I WOULD

_____

_____

_____

WHO CAME WITH ME

_____

_____

_____

_____

_____

DRAW AN EMJOI TO
DESCRIBE THE DAY

THIS CAMPING TRIP IN A _____
WAS _____ BECAUSE I GOT TO

_____

_____

I GIVE THIS TRIP  ☆ ☆ ☆ ☆

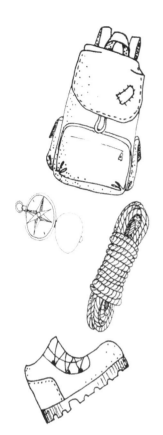

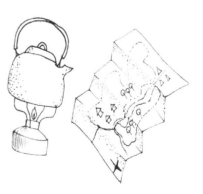

CAMPING AT _____

CAMPING IN A

TODAY'S DATE

WEATHER REPORT

BEST PART OF MY DAY

_____
_____
_____

WORST PART OF MY DAY

_____
_____
_____

TWO THINGS I LEARNED

_____
_____
_____
_____
_____
_____

TODAY WAS

AWESOME   FUN   COOL   TERRIFIC
OKAY   BORING   EXHAUSTING

CAMPING DOODLE

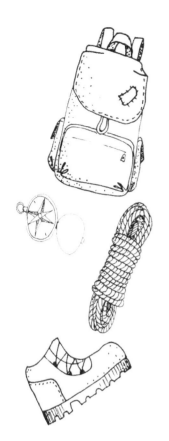

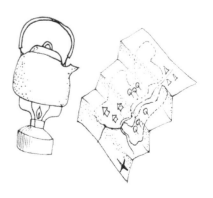

CAMPING AT _____

TODAY'S DATE

THREE THINGS I SAW TODAY

TODAY I ATE _____

WHO CAME WITH ME

AND IT TASTED    GREAT    AWESOME    HEAVENLY
                 HORRIBLE    TERRIBLE    OKAY

_____

_____

IF I WENT HERE AGAIN I WOULD

_____

_____

_____

_____

_____

_____

DRAW AN EMJOI TO
DESCRIBE THE DAY

THIS CAMPING TRIP IN A _____

WAS _____ BECAUSE I GOT TO

_____

_____

I GIVE THIS TRIP ☆ ☆ ☆ ☆

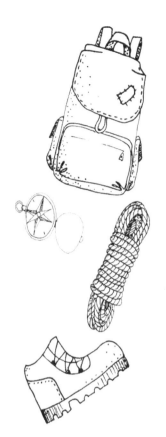

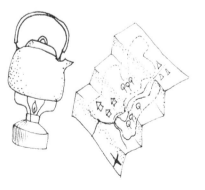

CAMPING AT _____

CAMPING IN A

TODAY'S DATE

WEATHER REPORT

BEST PART OF MY DAY
_____
_____
_____

WORST PART OF MY DAY
_____
_____
_____

TWO THINGS I LEARNED

_____
_____
_____
_____
_____
_____

TODAY WAS

AWESOME    FUN    COOL    TERRIFIC
OKAY    BORING    EXHAUSTING

CAMPING DOODLE

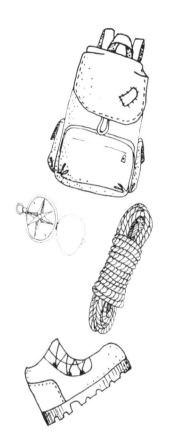

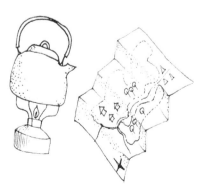

CAMPING AT _____

TODAY'S DATE

THREE THINGS I SAW TODAY

TODAY I ATE _____

AND IT TASTED   GREAT   AWESOME   HEAVENLY
                HORRIBLE   TERRIBLE   OKAY

WHO CAME WITH ME

_____

_____

_____

_____

IF I WENT HERE AGAIN I WOULD

_____

_____

_____

_____

DRAW AN EMJOI TO
DESCRIBE THE DAY

THIS CAMPING TRIP IN A _____
WAS _____ BECAUSE I GOT TO

_____

_____

I GIVE THIS TRIP ☆☆☆☆

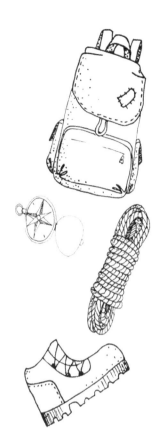

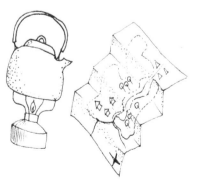

CAMPING AT _____

CAMPING IN A

TODAY'S DATE

BEST PART OF MY DAY

_____
_____
_____

WORST PART OF MY DAY

_____
_____
_____

WEATHER REPORT

TWO THINGS I LEARNED

_____
_____
_____
_____
_____
_____
_____

TODAY WAS

AWESOME   FUN   COOL   TERRIFIC
OKAY   BORING   EXHAUSTING

CAMPING DOODLE

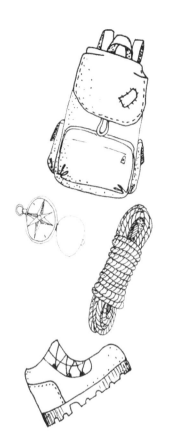

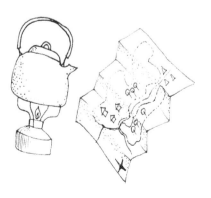

CAMPING AT _____

TODAY'S DATE

THREE THINGS I SAW TODAY

TODAY I ATE _____

WHO CAME WITH ME

AND IT TASTED   GREAT   AWESOME   HEAVENLY
                HORRIBLE   TERRIBLE   OKAY

IF I WENT HERE AGAIN I WOULD

DRAW AN EMJOI TO
DESCRIBE THE DAY

THIS CAMPING TRIP IN A _____
WAS _____ BECAUSE I GOT TO

I GIVE THIS TRIP ☆☆☆☆

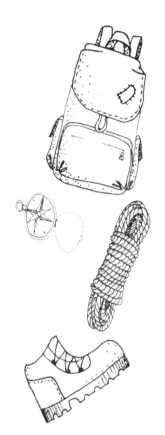

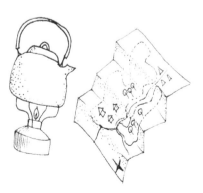

CAMPING AT _____

CAMPING IN A

WEATHER REPORT

BEST PART OF MY DAY
_____
_____
_____

WORST PART OF MY DAY
_____
_____
_____
_____

TWO THINGS I LEARNED

_____
_____
_____
_____
_____
_____
_____

TODAY WAS

AWESOME    FUN    COOL    TERRIFIC
OKAY    BORING    EXHAUSTING

CAMPING DOODLE

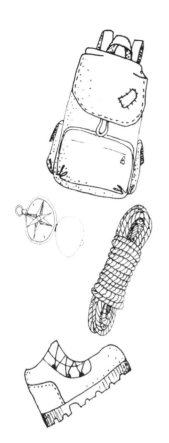

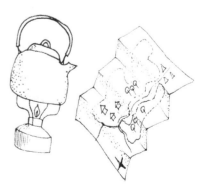

CAMPING AT _____

TODAY'S DATE

THREE THINGS I SAW TODAY

TODAY I ATE _____

AND IT TASTED    GREAT    AWESOME    HEAVENLY
                 HORRIBLE    TERRIBLE    OKAY

WHO CAME WITH ME

_____

_____

_____

_____

IF I WENT HERE AGAIN I WOULD

_____

_____

_____

_____

THIS CAMPING TRIP IN A _____

WAS _____ BECAUSE I GOT TO

_____

_____

DRAW AN EMJOI TO
DESCRIBE THE DAY

I GIVE THIS TRIP ☆☆☆☆

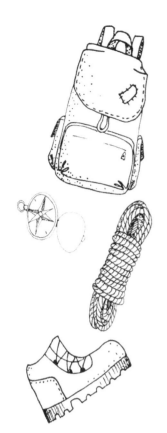

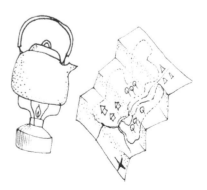

CAMPING AT _____

CAMPING IN A

WEATHER REPORT

BEST PART OF MY DAY
_____
_____
_____

WORST PART OF MY DAY
_____
_____
_____

TWO THINGS I LEARNED

_____
_____
_____
_____
_____
_____

TODAY WAS

AWESOME    FUN    COOL    TERRIFIC
OKAY    BORING    EXHAUSTING

CAMPING DOODLE

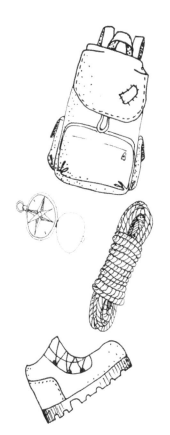

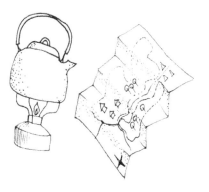

CAMPING AT _____

TODAY'S DATE

THREE THINGS I SAW TODAY

TODAY I ATE _____

AND IT TASTED  GREAT  AWESOME  HEAVENLY
               HORRIBLE  TERRIBLE  OKAY

IF I WENT HERE AGAIN I WOULD

_____

_____

_____

THIS CAMPING TRIP IN A _____

WAS _____ BECAUSE I GOT TO

_____

_____

WHO CAME WITH ME

_____

_____

_____

_____

_____

_____

DRAW AN EMJOI TO
DESCRIBE THE DAY

I GIVE THIS TRIP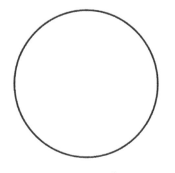

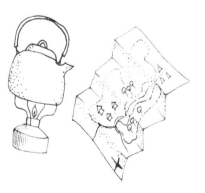

CAMPING AT _____

CAMPING IN A

BEST PART OF MY DAY

_____

_____

_____

WORST PART OF MY DAY

_____

_____

_____

WEATHER REPORT

TWO THINGS I LEARNED

_____

_____

_____

_____

_____

_____

_____

TODAY WAS

AWESOME    FUN    COOL    TERRIFIC

OKAY    BORING    EXHAUSTING

CAMPING DOODLE

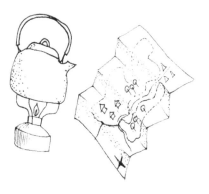

CAMPING AT _____

TODAY'S DATE

THREE THINGS I SAW TODAY

TODAY I ATE _____

AND IT TASTED GREAT AWESOME HEAVENLY
HORRIBLE TERRIBLE OKAY

IF I WENT HERE AGAIN I WOULD

WHO CAME WITH ME

DRAW AN EMJOI TO
DESCRIBE THE DAY

THIS CAMPING TRIP IN A _____
WAS _____ BECAUSE I GOT TO

I GIVE THIS TRIP ☆☆☆☆

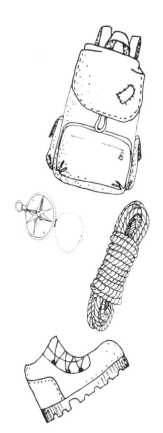

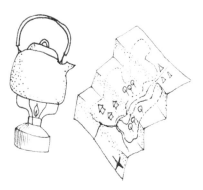

CAMPING AT _____

CAMPING IN A

WEATHER REPORT

BEST PART OF MY DAY
_____
_____
_____

WORST PART OF MY DAY
_____
_____
_____
_____

TWO THINGS I LEARNED

_____
_____
_____
_____
_____

TODAY WAS

AWESOME    FUN    COOL    TERRIFIC
OKAY    BORING    EXHAUSTING

CAMPING DOODLE

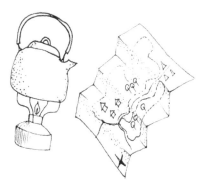

CAMPING AT _____

TODAY'S DATE

THREE THINGS I SAW TODAY

TODAY I ATE _____

AND IT TASTED    GREAT    AWESOME    HEAVENLY
                 HORRIBLE    TERRIBLE    OKAY

WHO CAME WITH ME

_____

_____

_____

_____

_____

IF I WENT HERE AGAIN I WOULD

_____

_____

_____

_____

DRAW AN EMJOI TO
DESCRIBE THE DAY

THIS CAMPING TRIP IN A _____
WAS _____ BECAUSE I GOT TO

_____

_____

I GIVE THIS TRIP ☆☆☆☆

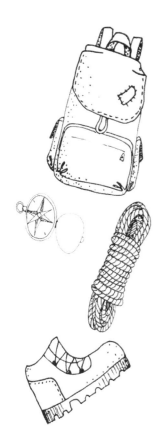

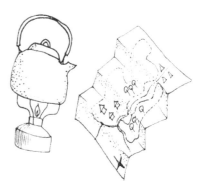

CAMPING AT _____

CAMPING IN A

TODAY'S DATE

WEATHER REPORT

BEST PART OF MY DAY
_____
_____
_____

WORST PART OF MY DAY
_____
_____
_____

TWO THINGS I LEARNED
_____
_____
_____
_____
_____
_____
_____

TODAY WAS

AWESOME    FUN    COOL    TERRIFIC
OKAY    BORING    EXHAUSTING

CAMPING DOODLE

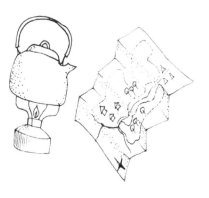

CAMPING AT _____

TODAY'S DATE

THREE THINGS I SAW TODAY

TODAY I ATE _____

AND IT TASTED  GREAT   AWESOME   HEAVENLY
               HORRIBLE   TERRIBLE   OKAY

IF I WENT HERE AGAIN I WOULD

_____

_____

_____

_____

WHO CAME WITH ME

_____

_____

_____

_____

_____

_____

DRAW AN EMJOI TO
DESCRIBE THE DAY

THIS CAMPING TRIP IN A _____

WAS _____ BECAUSE I GOT TO

_____

_____

I GIVE THIS TRIP ☆☆☆☆

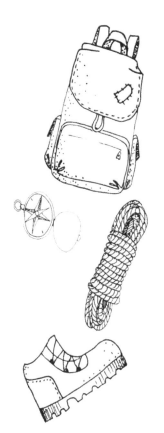

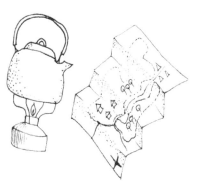

CAMPING AT _____

CAMPING IN A

TODAY'S DATE

WEATHER REPORT

BEST PART OF MY DAY
_____
_____
_____

WORST PART OF MY DAY
_____
_____
_____
_____

TWO THINGS I LEARNED

_____
_____
_____
_____
_____
_____
_____

TODAY WAS

AWESOME    FUN    COOL    TERRIFIC
OKAY    BORING    EXHAUSTING

CAMPING DOODLE

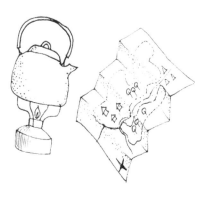

CAMPING AT _____

TODAY'S DATE

THREE THINGS I SAW TODAY

TODAY I ATE _____

AND IT TASTED  GREAT   AWESOME   HEAVENLY
               HORRIBLE   TERRIBLE   OKAY

IF I WENT HERE AGAIN I WOULD

_____
_____
_____
_____

WHO CAME WITH ME

_____
_____
_____
_____
_____
_____

DRAW AN EMJOI TO
DESCRIBE THE DAY

THIS CAMPING TRIP IN A _____
WAS _____ BECAUSE I GOT TO

_____
_____

I GIVE THIS TRIP ☆☆☆☆

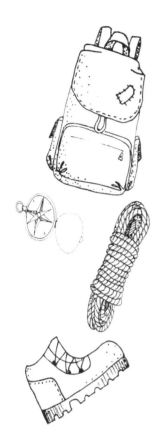

CAMPING AT _____

CAMPING IN A

BEST PART OF MY DAY

_____
_____
_____
_____

WORST PART OF MY DAY

_____
_____
_____
_____

WEATHER REPORT

TWO THINGS I LEARNED

_____
_____
_____
_____
_____
_____
_____
_____

TODAY WAS

AWESOME    FUN    COOL    TERRIFIC
OKAY    BORING    EXHAUSTING

CAMPING DOODLE

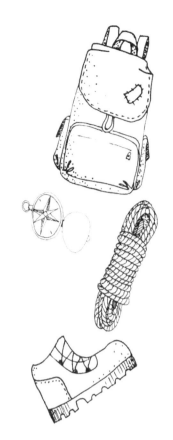

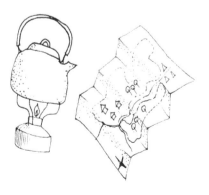

CAMPING AT _____

TODAY'S DATE

THREE THINGS I SAW TODAY

TODAY I ATE _____

AND IT TASTED  GREAT  AWESOME  HEAVENLY
HORRIBLE  TERRIBLE  OKAY

IF I WENT HERE AGAIN I WOULD

_____

_____

_____

_____

WHO CAME WITH ME

_____

_____

_____

_____

_____

DRAW AN EMJOI TO
DESCRIBE THE DAY

THIS CAMPING TRIP IN A _____
WAS _____ BECAUSE I GOT TO

_____

_____

I GIVE THIS TRIP ☆☆☆☆

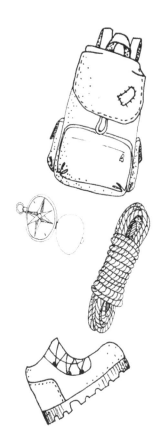

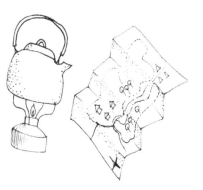

CAMPING AT _____

CAMPING IN A

WEATHER REPORT

BEST PART OF MY DAY

_____
_____
_____
_____

WORST PART OF MY DAY

_____
_____
_____
_____

TWO THINGS I LEARNED

_____
_____
_____
_____
_____
_____
_____
_____

TODAY WAS

AWESOME   FUN   COOL   TERRIFIC
OKAY   BORING   EXHAUSTING

CAMPING DOODLE

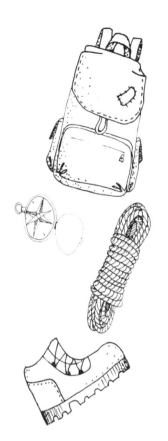

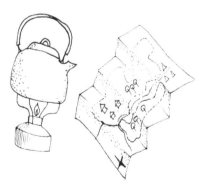

CAMPING AT _____

TODAY'S DATE

THREE THINGS I SAW TODAY

TODAY I ATE _____

AND IT TASTED   GREAT   AWESOME   HEAVENLY
                HORRIBLE   TERRIBLE   OKAY

IF I WENT HERE AGAIN I WOULD
_____
_____
_____
_____

WHO CAME WITH ME
_____
_____
_____
_____

DRAW AN EMJOI TO
DESCRIBE THE DAY

THIS CAMPING TRIP IN A _____
WAS _____ BECAUSE I GOT TO

_____

_____

I GIVE THIS TRIP

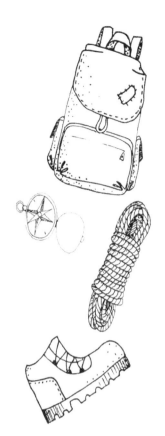

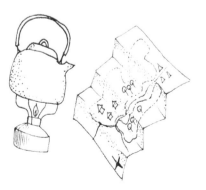

CAMPING AT _____

CAMPING IN A

TODAY'S DATE

WEATHER REPORT

BEST PART OF MY DAY

_____
_____
_____

WORST PART OF MY DAY

_____
_____
_____

TWO THINGS I LEARNED

_____
_____
_____
_____
_____
_____
_____

TODAY WAS

AWESOME    FUN    COOL    TERRIFIC
OKAY    BORING    EXHAUSTING

CAMPING DOODLE

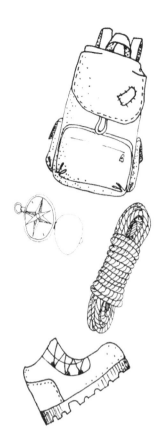

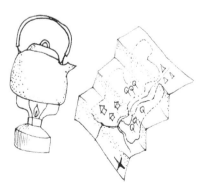

CAMPING AT _____

THREE THINGS I SAW TODAY

TODAY I ATE _____

AND IT TASTED    GREAT    AWESOME    HEAVENLY
                 HORRIBLE    TERRIBLE    OKAY

WHO CAME WITH ME

_____

_____

_____

_____

_____

IF I WENT HERE AGAIN I WOULD

_____

_____

_____

_____

DRAW AN EMJOI TO
DESCRIBE THE DAY

THIS CAMPING TRIP IN A _____

WAS _____ BECAUSE I GOT TO

_____

_____

I GIVE THIS TRIP  ☆☆☆☆

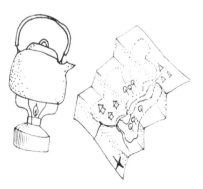

CAMPING AT _____

CAMPING IN A

TODAY'S DATE

WEATHER REPORT

BEST PART OF MY DAY
_____
_____
_____

WORST PART OF MY DAY
_____
_____
_____

TWO THINGS I LEARNED

TODAY WAS

AWESOME    FUN    COOL    TERRIFIC
OKAY    BORING    EXHAUSTING

CAMPING DOODLE

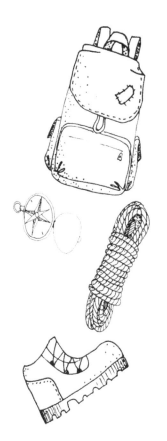

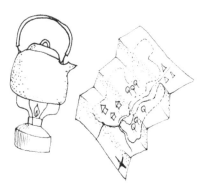

CAMPING AT _____

TODAY'S DATE _____

THREE THINGS I SAW TODAY

TODAY I ATE _____

AND IT TASTED    GREAT    AWESOME    HEAVENLY
                 HORRIBLE    TERRIBLE    OKAY

IF I WENT HERE AGAIN I WOULD

_____

_____

_____

_____

WHO CAME WITH ME

_____

_____

_____

_____

_____

DRAW AN EMJOI TO
DESCRIBE THE DAY

THIS CAMPING TRIP IN A _____
WAS _____ BECAUSE I GOT TO

_____

_____

I GIVE THIS TRIP  ☆ ☆ ☆ ☆

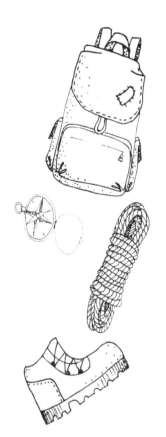

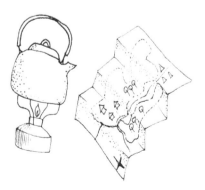

CAMPING AT _____

CAMPING IN A

TODAY'S DATE

BEST PART OF MY DAY
_____
_____
_____

WORST PART OF MY DAY
_____
_____
_____

WEATHER REPORT

TWO THINGS I LEARNED

_____
_____
_____
_____
_____
_____
_____

TODAY WAS

AWESOME    FUN    COOL    TERRIFIC
OKAY    BORING    EXHAUSTING

CAMPING DOODLE

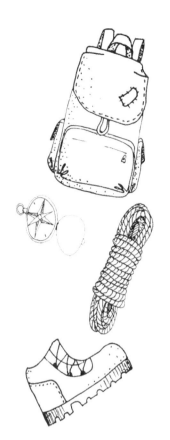

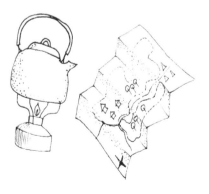

CAMPING AT _____

TODAY'S DATE _____

THREE THINGS I SAW TODAY

TODAY I ATE _____

AND IT TASTED GREAT AWESOME HEAVENLY
HORRIBLE TERRIBLE OKAY

IF I WENT HERE AGAIN I WOULD
_____
_____
_____
_____

WHO CAME WITH ME
_____
_____
_____
_____
_____

DRAW AN EMJOI TO
DESCRIBE THE DAY

THIS CAMPING TRIP IN A _____
WAS _____ BECAUSE I GOT TO
_____
_____

I GIVE THIS TRIP ☆☆☆☆

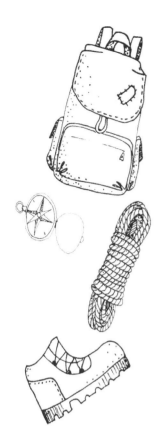

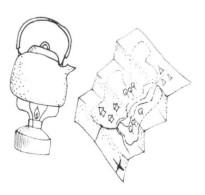

CAMPING AT _____

CAMPING IN A

TODAY'S DATE

WEATHER REPORT

BEST PART OF MY DAY

_____
_____
_____

WORST PART OF MY DAY

_____
_____
_____
_____

TWO THINGS I LEARNED

_____
_____
_____
_____
_____
_____
_____

TODAY WAS

AWESOME   FUN   COOL   TERRIFIC
OKAY   BORING   EXHAUSTING

CAMPING DOODLE

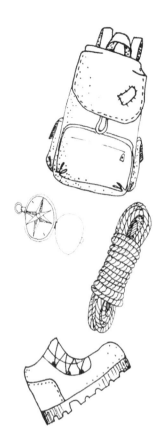

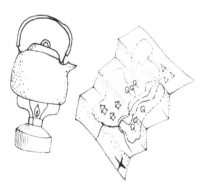

CAMPING AT _____

TODAY'S DATE

THREE THINGS I SAW TODAY

TODAY I ATE _____

AND IT TASTED    GREAT    AWESOME    HEAVENLY
                 HORRIBLE    TERRIBLE    OKAY

IF I WENT HERE AGAIN I WOULD

_____

_____

_____

WHO CAME WITH ME

_____

_____

_____

_____

_____

_____

DRAW AN EMJOI TO
DESCRIBE THE DAY

THIS CAMPING TRIP IN A _____
WAS _____ BECAUSE I GOT TO

_____

_____

I GIVE THIS TRIP ☆☆☆☆

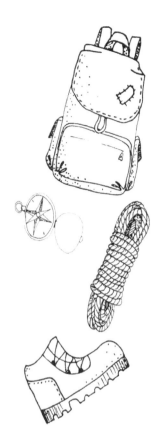

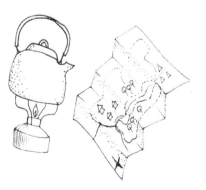

CAMPING AT _____
CAMPING IN A

TODAY'S DATE

WEATHER REPORT

BEST PART OF MY DAY
_____
_____
_____

WORST PART OF MY DAY
_____
_____
_____
_____

TWO THINGS I LEARNED

TODAY WAS

AWESOME    FUN    COOL    TERRIFIC
OKAY    BORING    EXHAUSTING

CAMPING DOODLE

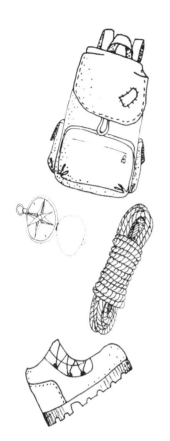

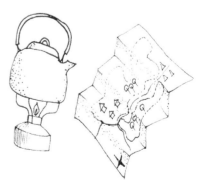

CAMPING AT _____

TODAY'S DATE

THREE THINGS I SAW TODAY

TODAY I ATE _____

AND IT TASTED    GREAT    AWESOME    HEAVENLY
                 HORRIBLE    TERRIBLE    OKAY

IF I WENT HERE AGAIN I WOULD
_____
_____
_____
_____

WHO CAME WITH ME
_____
_____
_____
_____
_____

DRAW AN EMJOI TO
DESCRIBE THE DAY

THIS CAMPING TRIP IN A _____
WAS _____ BECAUSE I GOT TO

_____

_____

I GIVE THIS TRIP ☆☆☆☆

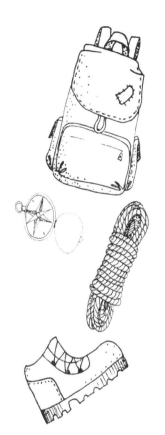

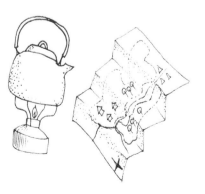

CAMPING AT _____

CAMPING IN A

TODAY'S DATE

## WEATHER REPORT

BEST PART OF MY DAY

_____
_____
_____

WORST PART OF MY DAY

_____
_____
_____
_____

TWO THINGS I LEARNED

_____
_____
_____
_____
_____
_____

TODAY WAS

AWESOME    FUN    COOL    TERRIFIC
OKAY    BORING    EXHAUSTING

CAMPING DOODLE

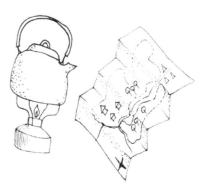

CAMPING AT _____

TODAY'S DATE

THREE THINGS I SAW TODAY

TODAY I ATE _____

AND IT TASTED   GREAT   AWESOME   HEAVENLY
                HORRIBLE   TERRIBLE   OKAY

IF I WENT HERE AGAIN I WOULD

_____

_____

_____

WHO CAME WITH ME

_____

_____

_____

_____

_____

_____

DRAW AN EMJOI TO
DESCRIBE THE DAY

THIS CAMPING TRIP IN A _____
WAS _____ BECAUSE I GOT TO

_____

_____

I GIVE THIS TRIP ☆ ☆ ☆ ☆

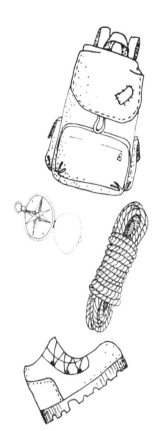

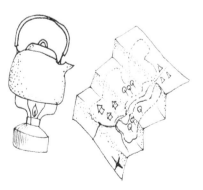

CAMPING AT _____

CAMPING IN A

TODAY'S DATE

BEST PART OF MY DAY

_____
_____
_____
_____

WORST PART OF MY DAY

_____
_____
_____
_____

WEATHER REPORT

TWO THINGS I LEARNED

_____
_____
_____
_____
_____
_____
_____
_____

TODAY WAS

AWESOME   FUN   COOL   TERRIFIC
OKAY   BORING   EXHAUSTING

CAMPING DOODLE

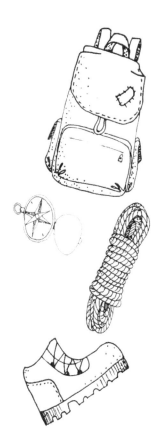

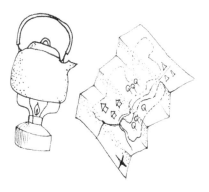

CAMPING AT _____

THREE THINGS I SAW TODAY

TODAY I ATE _____

AND IT TASTED    GREAT    AWESOME    HEAVENLY
                 HORRIBLE    TERRIBLE    OKAY

IF I WENT HERE AGAIN I WOULD

_____
_____
_____

WHO CAME WITH ME

_____
_____
_____
_____

DRAW AN EMJOI TO
DESCRIBE THE DAY

THIS CAMPING TRIP IN A _____
WAS _____ BECAUSE I GOT TO

_____
_____

I GIVE THIS TRIP ☆☆☆☆

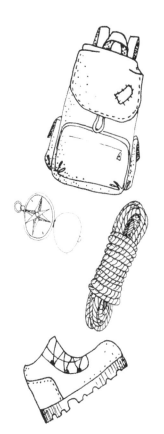

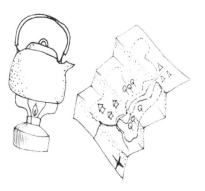

CAMPING AT _____

CAMPING IN A

TODAY'S DATE

WEATHER REPORT

BEST PART OF MY DAY
_____
_____
_____

WORST PART OF MY DAY
_____
_____
_____
_____

TWO THINGS I LEARNED

_____
_____
_____
_____
_____
_____
_____

TODAY WAS

AWESOME    FUN    COOL    TERRIFIC
OKAY    BORING    EXHAUSTING

CAMPING DOODLE

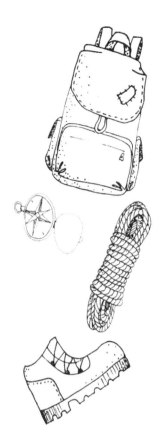

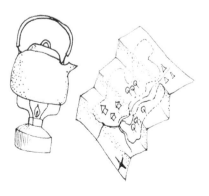

CAMPING AT _____          TODAY'S DATE

THREE THINGS I SAW TODAY

TODAY I ATE _____

AND IT TASTED   GREAT   AWESOME   HEAVENLY
                HORRIBLE   TERRIBLE   OKAY

WHO CAME WITH ME

IF I WENT HERE AGAIN I WOULD

DRAW AN EMJOI TO
DESCRIBE THE DAY

THIS CAMPING TRIP IN A _____
WAS _____ BECAUSE I GOT TO

I GIVE THIS TRIP ☆☆☆☆

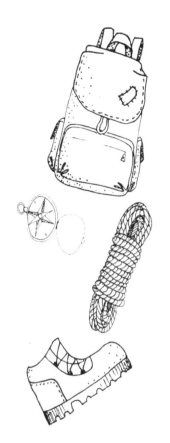

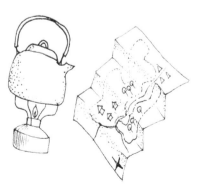

Made in the USA
Monee, IL
06 June 2021